JAMESTOWN EDUCATION

English, Yes!

Learning English Through Literature

Level 1: Basic

McGraw Hill **Glencoe**

New York, New York   Columbus, Ohio   Chicago, Illinois   Peoria, Illinois   Woodland Hills, California

Acknowledgments

Acknowledgment is gratefully made to the following publishers, authors, and agents for permission to reprint these works.

"Saying Yes" by Diana Chang. Reprinted by permission of the author.

Excerpt from "New Shoes" by Peter and Ellen Allard. Copyright © 1997 by Peter & Ellen Allard. All rights reserved. Reprinted by permission.

Excerpt from "Blueberries" from *The Poetry of Robert Frost,* edited by Edward Connery Lathem. Copyright 1930, 1939, © 1969 by Henry Holt and Co., © 1958 by Robert Frost, © 1967 by Lesley Frost Ballantine. Reprinted by permission of Henry Holt and Company, LLC.

"Celebration" by Alonzo Lopez, from *Whispering Wind* by Terry Allen, copyright © 1972 by the Institute of American Indian Arts. Used by permission of Doubleday, a division of Random House, Inc.

"The Quarrel" from *Eleanor Farjeon's Poems for Children,* by Eleanor Farjeon. Copyright © 1933, 1961 by Eleanor Farjeon. Reprinted by permission of Harold Ober Associates Incorporated.

Photo Credits

iv Alison McKinzie; **11** PhotoDisc; **(br)** Chuck Savage/CORBIS; **21** PhotoDisc; **31** Gail Mooney/CORBIS; **(br)** Corbis Royalty Free; **41** PhotoDisc; **51** PhotoDisc; **(br)** Steve Kaufman/CORBIS; **61** PhotoDisc; **71** Creatas; **(br)** Alison McKinzie; **81** PhotoDisc.

Cover photo illustration: Third Eye Image/Solus Photography/Veer.

Glencoe

The McGraw-Hill Companies

Send all inquiries to:
Glencoe/McGraw-Hill
8787 Orion Place
Columbus, OH 43240-4027

ISBN 0-07-831108-X
Printed in the United States of America.

4 5 6 7 8 9 10 021 08 07 06 05

Contents

Getting Started

Words and numbers are everywhere.
We use them to talk, to read, and to write.

Words and numbers help us understand our world.
Let's start by reviewing letters and numbers.

THE ALPHABET

Study the capital letters below.

A B C D E F G H I J K L M N

O P Q R S T U V W X Y Z

B. Finding Capital Letters

Circle. The first two have been done for you.

A	B	(A)	J	K
E	D	E	F	R
C	C	O	D	G
S	R	P	B	S
R	P	B	R	S

W	X	V	(W)	K
M	M	N	W	Y
T	L	F	E	T
B	R	H	E	B
V	W	Y	V	J

C. Finding Capital Letters

Match. The first one has been done for you.

A   V

B   R

V   A

K   G

G   B

R   K

D. Finding Capital Letters

Circle. The first two have been done for you.

T	（T）ELEPHONE	S（T）UDENT	STATE
L	LAST	NICKEL	DOLLAR
I	CITY	SHIRT	TIME
F	LEFT	FRIDAY	FIFTEEN
E	NAME	STREET	TEACHER
K	WEEK	SKIRT	JACKET

E. Writing Capital Letters

Write.

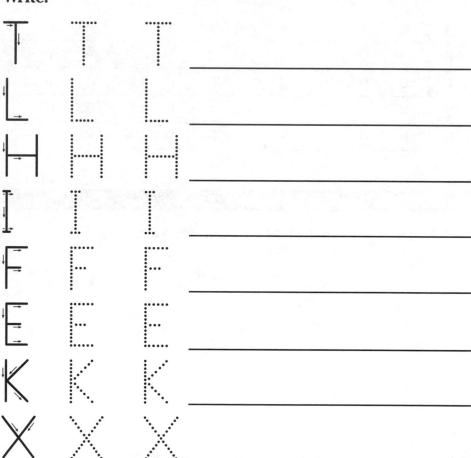

F. Finding Capital Letters

Circle. The first one has been done for you.

V	FI(V)E	MOVIES	VEGETABLE
A	NAME	ART	JACKET
M	MATH	DIME	GYM
N	JEANS	LUNCH	TEN
W	SWEATER	TWO	WHITE
Y	YES	MAY	HISTORY

G. Writing Capital Letters

Write.

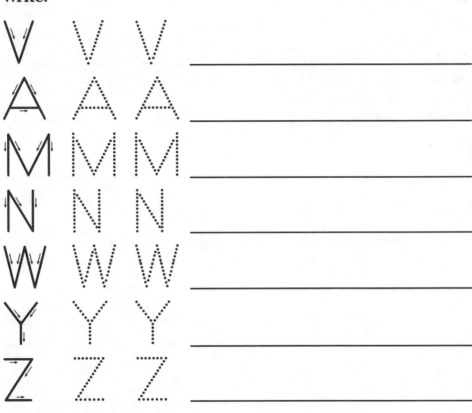

H. Finding Capital Letters

Circle. The first one has been done for you.

C	ⒸLASS	JACKET	BLACK
S	BEANS	STREET	FISH
D	MONDAY	DIME	SALAD
R	NUMBER	RED	LARGE
P	POOL	PANTS	APPLE
B	JOB	BOOTS	LIBRARY

I. Writing Capital Letters

Write.

O O O _____

Q Q Q _____

C C C _____

G G G _____

U U U _____

S S S _____

D D D _____

P P P _____

B B B _____

R R R _____

J. Capital Letters and Small Letters

Study the capital letters and small letters.

Aa	Bb	Cc	Dd	Ee	Ff	Gg	Hh	Ii
Jj	Kk	Ll	Mm	Nn	Oo	Pp	Qq	Rr
Ss	Tt	Uu	Vv	Ww	Kx	Yy	Zz	

K. Finding Small Letters

Circle. The first one has been done for you.

a	o	ⓐ	c	g
f	f	r	e	a
c	c	o	d	g
s	r	p	b	s
t	k	l	f	t

n	h	w	n	x
m	m	n	w	y
r	n	r	e	m
b	r	h	e	b
v	w	y	v	x

L. Finding Small Letters

Match. The first one has been done for you.

A   d

B   p

D   r

G   a

M   t

P   b

R   g

T   m

M. Writing Small Letters

Write.

a	a	_____	**h**	h	_____
b	b	_____	**i**	i	_____
c	c	_____	**j**	j	_____
d	d	_____	**k**	k	_____
e	e	_____	**l**	l	_____
f	f	_____	**m**	m	_____
g	g	_____	**n**	n	_____

N. Writing Small Letters

Complete the words. Write the letters.
The first one has been done for you.

bread

_b_ read

dime

___ ime

nickel

___ ickel

cake

___ ake

eggs

___ ggs

apple

___ pple

O. Writing Small Letters

Write.

o	o	_____	**u**	u	_____
p	p	_____	**v**	v	_____
q	q	_____	**w**	w	_____
r	r	_____	**x**	x	_____
s	s	_____	**y**	y	_____
t	t	_____	**z**	z	_____

P. Writing Small Letters

Complete the words. Write the letters.

pants

___ ants

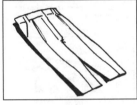

shirt

___ hirt

women's shoes

___ omen's shoes

rice

___ ice

orange

___ range

vegetables

___ egetables

Q. Writing Small Letters

Complete the words. Write the letters.

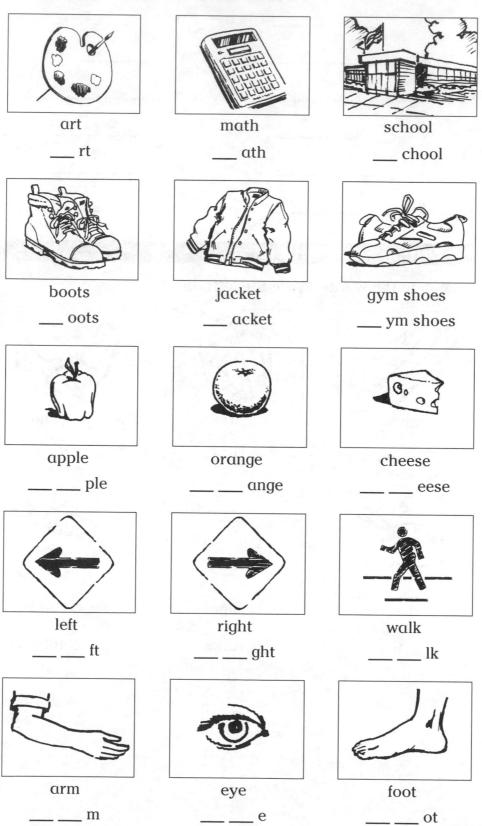

art

___ rt

math

___ ath

school

___ chool

boots

___ oots

jacket

___ acket

gym shoes

___ ym shoes

apple

___ ___ ple

orange

___ ___ ange

cheese

___ ___ eese

left

___ ___ ft

right

___ ___ ght

walk

___ ___ lk

arm

___ ___ m

eye

___ ___ e

foot

___ ___ ot

Write the words.

street

city

telephone

_____

music

gym

English

_____

socks

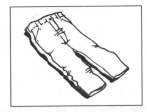

jeans

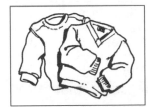

sweaters

_____

carrot

potato

sandwich

_____

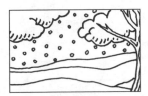

snowy

sunny

cloudy

_____

NUMBERS

A. Learning Numbers

Study the numbers below.

one	two	three	four	five	six
1	2	3	4	5	6

seven	eight	nine	ten	eleven	twelve
7	8	9	10	11	12

B. Finding Numbers

Circle. The first one has been done for you.

one	2	3	4	(1)
two	9	8	2	5
three	8	3	5	6
four	9	8	4	5

six	8	6	9	1
eight	7	9	4	8
eleven	10	12	11	1
twelve	1	2	12	10

C. Finding Numbers

Match. The first one has been done for you.

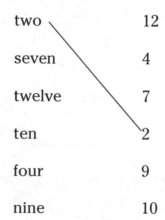

two   12

seven   4

twelve   7

ten   2

four   9

nine   10

Who Am I?

We come from many places.
We are all different.
But we are all citizens of the world.

Your teacher will read aloud this poem about
being both Chinese and American.
Listen and follow along.

Saying Yes
by Diana Chang

"Are you Chinese?"
"Yes."

"American?"
"Yes."

"*Really* Chinese?"
"No . . . not quite."

"*Really* American?"
"Well, actually, you see . . . "

But I would rather say
yes

Not neither-nor,
not maybe,
but both, and not only

The homes I've had,
the ways I am

I'd rather say it
twice,
yes

READING SCHOOL ID CARDS AND FORMS.

Read the school ID cards and student form below.

Horton School Student Identification

Name <u>Ana</u>   <u>Sanchez</u>
      first   last

Homeroom   <u>329</u>

Horton School Teacher Identification

Name <u>Mr. Gomez</u>

Room <u>329</u>

Student Form

Name   <u>Ana</u>   <u>Sanchez</u>
     first   last

Address   <u>100 Wood Street</u>
             street

            <u>Davenport, Iowa 52802</u>
            city   state   zip code

Telephone number <u>555-9493</u>

WORDS TO LEARN

Study the words.

Name Words

My first name is Ana.
My last name is Sanchez.

name   first name   last name

Titles

Mr.   Miss or Ms.   Mrs. or Ms.

Note: Use titles before names and last names.
Mr. Juan Gomez, Mr. Gomez

School Words

student   teacher   school

Personal Information Words

address   city   state
street   zip code (60611)

telephone
telephone number
555-1479

COMPREHENSION AND VOCABULARY

A. Checking Your Understanding

Put an x in the box next to the correct answer. The first one has been done for you.

1. The first name of
   Ana Sanchez is
   ☒ Ana.
   ❏ Sanchez.

2. The last name of
   Juan Gomez is
   ❏ Juan.
   ❏ Gomez.

3. <u>Ana Sanchez</u>
   Sanchez is her
   ❏ first name.
   ❏ last name.

4. <u>Juan Gomez</u>
   Gomez is his
   ❏ first name.
   ❏ last name.

5. Ana Sanchez is a
   ❏ teacher.
   ❏ student.

6. Juan Gomez is a
   ❏ teacher.
   ❏ student.

7. Ana's address is
   ❏ 555-9403.
   ❏ 100 Wood Street.

8.
   ❏ street
   ❏ telephone

9.
   ❏ street
   ❏ city

10.
    ❏ school
    ❏ state

How many questions did you answer correctly? Circle your score. Then fill in your score on the Score Chart on page 91.

Number Correct	1	2	3	4	5	6	7	8	9	10
Score	10	20	30	40	50	60	70	80	90	100

B. Practicing Vocabulary: Finding Words

Circle. The first one has been done for you.

1. FIRST	FOREST	(FIRST)	FROST
2. LAST	LIST	LEFT	LAST
3. NAME	TAME	NAME	FAME
4. first	film	fist	first
5. last	lift	last	lost
6. name	none	same	name

C. Practicing Vocabulary: Finding Letters

1. Circle the letters in Ana's last name. One letter has been done for you.

Ana Sanchez

Ⓐ B C D E F G H I J K L M

N O P Q R S T U V W X Y Z

2. Circle the letters in Mr. Gomez's first name.

Juan Gomez

A B C D E F G H I J K L M

N O P Q R S T U V W X Y Z

3. What letters are in your first name? Circle them.

A B C D E F G H I J K L M

N O P Q R S T U V W X Y Z

TRY IT

Say the letters in your first and last names.

Match. The first one has been done for you.

Mark Jones

1. Name —————— Mark
2. First name ——— Mark Jones
3. Last name   Jones

Linda Lake

1. Name   Lake
2. First name Linda
3. Last name   Linda Lake

E. Using Vocabulary: Name Words

Complete the forms. Use the names.

Tom Chang

Name		
first		last

Julia Post

Name		
first		last

TRY IT

Complete the form. Use your name.

Name		
first		last

Match. The first one has been done for you.

My name is Luther Silverwolf.
My address is 109 State
Street, Chicago, Illinois.
My zip code is 60006.

Street   Luther Silverwolf   Zip Code

Name   109 State Street   City

State   Chicago, Illinois 60006

My name is Radha Gupta.
My address is 356 Ocean Street,
San Jose, California.
My zip code is 95123.

San
Jose   Name   *Radha*   Radha
               first   last

Gupta   Address   356 Ocean
               street   Street

                              95123
               city   state   zip

Circle. The first one has been done for you.

1. Lily **Lee**   first name   (last name)

2. 555-5790   telephone number   zip code

3. 145 Green Street   street   city

4. 95838   zip code   telephone number

5. California   city   state

H. Understanding Vocabulary: Telephone Numbers

Complete the form. The first one has been done for you.

My name is Maria Reyes.
My telephone number is 555-9419.

My name is Viktor Chernov.
My telephone number is 555-6135.

Name _Maria_____   _____
      first   last

Telephone number _____

Name _____   _Chernov_____
      first   last

Telephone number _____

Complete the form. One blank has been filled for you.

Name _____ *Johnson* _____
         first   last

Address_____
         street

_____   _____   _____
      city   state   zip code

Telephone number_____

WRAP-UP: WRITING AND SHARING

A. Write about yourself.

Name _____
           first   last

Address _____
           street

_____
           city   state   zip code

Telephone number _____

B. Write about your school.

School name _____

Address _____
           street

_____
           city   state   zip code

Telephone number _____

C. Write the names of three students.

_____
first name   last name

_____
first name   last name

_____
first name   last name

Going Places

Days go by quickly.
There are so many things to do.
How do you spend your time?

Your teacher will read aloud this poem about time.
Listen and follow along.

How Many Seconds?
by Christina Rossetti

How many seconds in a minute?
Sixty, and no more in it.

How many minutes in an hour?
Sixty for sun and shower.

How many hours in a day?
Twenty-four for work and play.

How many days in a week?
Seven both to hear and speak.

How many weeks in a month?
Four, as the swift moon runn'th.

How many months in a year?
Twelve the almanack makes clear.

How many years in an age?
One hundred says the sage.

How many ages in time?
No one knows the rhyme.

READING SCHEDULES

Read Ana's schedule.

Ana's Schedule

	Monday	Tuesday	Wednesday	Thursday	Friday	Saturday	Sunday
8:00 A.M.	math	math	math	math	math		
9:00	ESL	ESL	ESL	ESL	ESL		
10:00	art	music	art	music	art	pool	
11:00	history	geography	history	geography	history		church
12:00 P.M.	lunch	lunch	lunch	lunch	lunch		
1:00	English	English	English	English	English		
2:00	library	library	library	library	library	mall	
3:00	gym	gym	gym	gym	gym		
4:00							
5:00	job		job		job		movies

On weekdays Ana goes to school.
Her first class is at 8 o'clock in the morning.
She goes to her job on Monday, Wednesday, and Friday.
On weekends Ana does not go to school or to her job.

Note:
weekends = Saturday and Sunday
weekdays = Monday, Tuesday, Wednesday, Thursday, Friday

A.M. = morning, before noon
P.M. = afternoon, after noon
8 o'clock = 8:00

WORDS TO LEARN

Study the words.

Subjects

math

English

art

history

geography

gym

music

ESL

Places

library

pool

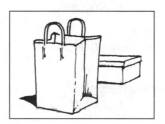
mall

church

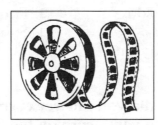
movies

Days of the Week

Monday	Tuesday	Wednesday	Thursday
Friday	Saturday	Sunday	

COMPREHENSION AND VOCABULARY

Put an *x* in the box next to the correct answer. The first one has been done for you.

1. Ana has math class at
   - ❏ 7:00 A.M.
   - ☒ 8:00 A.M.

2. Ana has lunch at
   - ❏ 10:00 A.M.
   - ❏ 12:00 P.M.

3. Ana has gym at
   - ❏ 2:00 P.M.
   - ❏ 3:00 P.M.

4. Ana goes to church on
   - ❏ Monday.
   - ❏ Sunday.

5. Ana goes to the pool on
   - ❏ Sunday.
   - ❏ Saturday.

6. Ana's job is on
   - ❏ Monday, Wednesday, and Friday.
   - ❏ Monday, Tuesday, and Thursday.

7.
   - ❏ history
   - ❏ math

8.
   - ❏ music
   - ❏ geography

9. day of the week
   - ❏ English
   - ❏ Wednesday

10. weekend
    - ❏ Friday and Saturday
    - ❏ Saturday and Sunday

How many questions did you answer correctly? Circle your score. Then fill in your score on the Score Chart on page 91.

Number Correct	1	2	3	4	5	6	7	8	9	10
Score	10	20	30	40	50	60	70	80	90	100

Match. The first one has been done for you.

1. pool

2. mall

3. library

4. movies

5. church

Complete the words. The first one has been done for you.

1.

E *nglish* _____

2.

G _____

3.

A _____

4.

M _____

Circle. The first one has been done for you.

1.   1:00   6:00   (8:00)

2.   9:00   10:00   11:00

3.   3:00   4:00   5:00

4.   11:00   12:00   1:00

Write the times.

_____   _____   _____   _____   _____

TRY IT

Work with a partner. Repeat the conversation.

What time is it?

Thank you.

It's 9 o'clock.

E. Learning Vocabulary: Days of the Week

Sunday	Monday	Tuesday	Wednesday	Thursday	Friday	Saturday
1	2	3	4	5	6	7
8	9	10	11	12	13	14
15	16	17	18	19	20	21
22	23	24	25	26	27	28
29	30	31				

What day is it? Use the calendar. Circle. The first two have been done for you.

1	(Sunday)	Tuesday	Monday
5	Tuesday	Wednesday	(Thursday)
2	Monday	Tuesday	Saturday
7	Saturday	Sunday	Thursday
8	Sunday	Monday	Tuesday
12	Friday	Thursday	Sunday

What day is it? Use the calendar. Write. The first one has been done for you.

3 _____Tuesday_____

10 _____

13 _____

22 _____

Complete the schedule. Use the information in the box.

	Monday	Tuesday	Wednesday	Thursday	Friday
8:00 A.M.					
9:00					
10:00					
11:00					
12:00 P.M.					
1:00					
2:00	*gym*	*gym*	*gym*	*gym*	*gym*

Monday, Tuesday, Wednesday, Thursday, Friday

gym at 2:00　　lunch at 11:00
English at 8:00　history at 12:00
math at 9:00　　library at 1:00

Tuesday, Thursday
art at 10:00

Monday, Wednesday, Friday
music at 10:00

G. Vocabulary Review

Write the missing word. The first one has been done for you.

1. Monday, ____*Tuesday*____, Wednesday

2. Sunday, _____, Tuesday

3. Thursday, _____, Saturday

4. Wednesday, _____, Friday

5. Saturday, _____, Monday

Lisa's schedule.

	Monday	Tuesday	Wednesday	Thursday	Friday	Saturday	Sunday
8:00 A.M.							
9:00	ESL	ESL	ESL	ESL	ESL	job	
10:00	English	English	English	English	English		
11:00							
12:00 P.M.	lunch	lunch	lunch	lunch	lunch		
1:00	history	geography	history	geography	history		
2:00	library	library	library	library	library		
3:00	art	music	art	music	art		
4:00							
5:00	pool		pool			movies	

Write. The first one has been done for you

1. Lisa has English class at ___10:00___.

2. Lisa goes to the library at _____.

3. Lisa has lunch at _____.

4. Lisa has music class on Tuesday and _____.

5. Lisa has history class on Monday, Wednesday, and

   _____.

Read the conversations. Complete Lisa's schedule above.

WRAP-UP: WRITING AND SHARING

A. Write your schedule.

	Monday	Tuesday	Wednesday	Thursday	Friday	Saturday	Sunday
8:00 A.M.							
9:00							
10:00							
11:00							
12:00 P.M.							
1:00							
2:00							
3:00							
4:00							
5:00							
6:00							
7:00							

B. Talk about your schedule with a partner. Use questions like the ones in the pictures on page 29.

Unit 3 SHOPPING

Let's Go Shopping

Some people love to shop.
Others think it is a bore.
Either way, shopping is something we all do.

Your teacher will read aloud this song about
shopping for new shoes.
Listen and follow along.

New Shoes
by Peter and Ellen Allard

All of a sudden I saw them,
The sneakers that had to be mine,
In all of my life I had never
seen foot coverings so fine.
The sneakers called out my name from the window
Where they'd been living for almost a week,
Please take me home I need rescue,
From this shelf in this shoe boutique.

READING CLOTHING ADS

Look at the clothes on sale.

jeans
$22.00
S, M, L, XL
blue, black

jackets
$30.00
S, M, L, XL
black, brown, blue

shirts
$12.00
S, M, L, XL
assorted colors

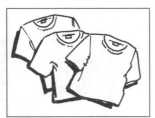

T-shirts
$9.00
S, M, L, XL
assorted colors

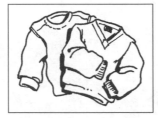

sweaters
$24.00
S, M, L, XL
white, red, blue

socks
$1.99
S, L
white

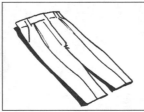

men's pants
$28.50
S, M, L
blue, brown, black

women's skirts
$19.00
S, M, L, XL
blue, green, black

women's shoes
$42.00
all sizes
assorted colors

gym shoes
$49.90
all sizes
white

boots
$19.00
all sizes
blue, brown, black

Note:
99=ninety-nine
24=twenty-four
assorted colors=
many different
colors

WORDS TO LEARN

Study the words.

Clothing

boots	jacket	jeans	pants	shirt
shoes	skirt	sweater	socks	T-shirt

Colors

blue	brown	black
green	red	white

Sizes

small S	medium M	large L	extra large XL

Money

penny	nickel	dime	quarter
1¢	5¢	10¢	25¢
$.01	$.05	$.10	$.25

one-dollar bill	five-dollar bill	ten-dollar bill	twenty-dollar
$1.00	$5.00	$10.00	bill $20.00

More Numbers

thirteen	13	twenty	20
fourteen	14	thirty	30
fifteen	15	forty	40
sixteen	16	fifty	50
seventeen	17	sixty	60
eighteen	18	seventy	70
nineteen	19	eighty	80
		ninety	90

COMPREHENSION AND VOCABULARY

A. Checking Your Understanding

Put an *x* in the box next to the correct answer.

1. The price of jeans is
   - ❏ $22.00.
   - ❏ $29.99.

2. The price of a
   T-shirt is
   - ❏ $9.00.
   - ❏ $19.00.

3. $24.00 is the price
   of the
   - ❏ shirts.
   - ❏ sweaters.

4. Jeans come in
   - ❏ black and blue.
   - ❏ blue and red.

5. Shirts come in
   - ❏ white only.
   - ❏ assorted colors.

6. Jackets come in
   - ❏ sizes S, M, L, and XL.
   - ❏ sizes M, L, and XL.

7. The sale is for
   - ❏ party clothes.
   - ❏ school clothes.

8. *Size M* means
   - ❏ small.
   - ❏ medium.

9. *Assorted colors*
   means
   - ❏ one color.
   - ❏ many different colors.

10. A *sale* means
    - ❏ no prices.
    - ❏ lower prices.

**How many questions did you answer correctly? Circle
your score. Then fill in your score on the Score Chart
on page 91.**

Number Correct	1	2	3	4	5	6	7	8	9	10
Score	10	20	30	40	50	60	70	80	90	100

B. Practicing Vocabulary: Clothing

Complete the sentences. Use words from the box. The first one has been done for you.

boots	gym shoes
jacket	skirt
jeans	sweater
pants	socks
shirt	T-shirt

1.  This _sweater_ costs $24.

2.  These _____ come in blue or black.

3.  These _____ are on sale.

4.  Are these _____ on sale?

5.  How much are these _____ ?

6.  Does this _____ come in extra large?

7.  This _____ is a medium size.

8.  How much is this _____ ?

9.  These _____ are on sale, too.

10.  This _____ comes in assorted colors.

C. Practicing Vocabulary: Numbers

Write the numbers. The first one has been done for you.

20   _twenty_

30   _____

50   _____

70   _____

24   _____ _-four_

32   _____ _-two_

65   _____ _-five_

D. Practicing Vocabulary: Money

Match. Draw lines. The first one has been done for you.

1. quarter $.10

2. penny $.05

3. dime $.25

4. nickel $.01

E. Counting Money

Count the money. Circle.

1. $1.75
   $5.40
   $1.45

2. $2.00
   $2.10
   $2.01

3. $20.51
   $21.20
   $21.50

4. $1.75
   $5.40
   $1.45

5. $10.87
   $10.78
   $10.85

F. Counting Money

Count the money. Write. The first one has been done for you.

1. _$3.25_

2. _____

3. _____

4. _____

5. _____

Complete the conversations. Use the information in the boxes.

Clothing	Price	Size
![jacket]	$30	L

Clothing	Price	Size
![pants]	$22	S

Complete the conversations. Use the information in the box.

| jacket $30 | T-shirt $9 | jeans $22 | sweater $24 |

1.

Customer: How much are these _____?

Clerk: They're _____.

Customer: Here's _____.

Clerk: Your change is _____.

2.

Customer: How much is this _____?

Clerk: It's _____.

Customer: Here's _____.

Clerk: Your change is _____.

3.

Customer: How much are these _____?

Clerk: They're _____.

Customer: Here's _____.

Clerk: Your change is _____.

TRY IT

Work with a partner. Repeat the conversations.

WRAP-UP: WRITING AND SHARING

A. What clothes are you wearing now? Make a list.

Ideas:
a T-shirt   a green T-shirt
a jacket   a black jacket
jeans   blue jeans

_____

_____

_____

_____

Share your list with a partner.

B. What are your favorite clothes? Make a list.

_____

_____

_____

_____

Talk with a partner. Tell about your favorite clothes.

Food, Glorious Food

What meal do you like best?
What's your favorite food?

Your teacher will read aloud this poem
about one person's favorite food.
Listen and follow along.

Blueberries
by Robert Frost

You ought to have seen what I saw on my way
To the village, through Mortenson's pasture to-day:
Blueberries as big as the end of your thumb,
Real sky-blue, and heavy, and ready to drum
In the cavernous pail of the first one to come!
And all ripe together, not some of them green
And some of them ripe! You ought to have seen!

STUDYING A FOOD PYRAMID

Study the food pyramid. Read the information below it.

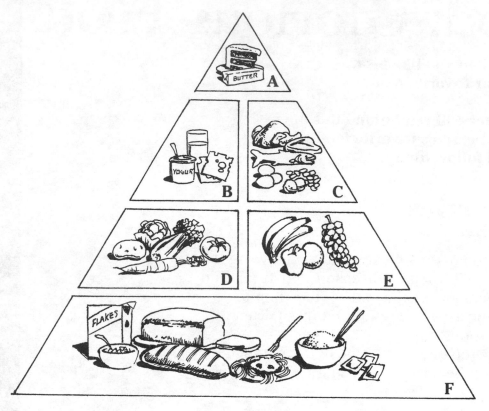

Food Pyramid

A. Sweets and fats
Do not eat a lot of these.

B. Meat, poultry, fish, eggs
2–3 servings every day

C. Fruit
2–4 servings every day

D. Milk and cheese
2–3 servings every day

E. Vegetables
3–5 servings every day

F. Bread, cereal, rice, pasta
6–11 servings every day

The pyramid shows the right foods to eat every day.

Meals

In the United States, many people eat three meals every day.
1. Breakfast is in the morning. (6:00–9:00 A.M.)
2. Lunch is in the afternoon. (12:00–2:00 P.M.)
3. Dinner is in the evening. (5:00–8:00 P.M.)

Lunch and dinner often have three parts:
1. soup or salad
2. meat and vegetables
3. dessert (Dessert often is cake or ice cream.)

WORDS TO LEARN

Study the words.

Fruit

apple   banana   lemon   orange   peach   strawberry

Vegetables

tomato   lettuce   carrot   cucumber   potato   beans

Meat

chicken   hamburger   steak

Other Foods

bread   cake   cereal   cheese   eggs   fish

pasta   rice   salad   sandwich   soup

Beverages

milk   juice

Meals/Parts of Meals

breakfast   lunch   dinner   dessert

COMPREHENSION AND VOCABULARY

A. Checking Your Understanding

Put an x in the box next to the correct answer.

1. Every day try to eat 2–4 servings of
   - ❏ meat.
   - ❏ fruit.

2. Every day try to eat 3–5 servings of
   - ❏ sweets.
   - ❏ vegetables.

3. Do not eat a lot of
   - ❏ sweets.
   - ❏ rice.

4. For bread, cereal, rice, and pasta, try to eat
   - ❏ 2–3 servings.
   - ❏ 6–11 servings.

5. You eat breakfast in the
   - ❏ morning.
   - ❏ afternoon.

6. In the United States, many people eat
   - ❏ three meals every day.
   - ❏ one meal every day.

7. Dessert is often
   - ❏ cake or ice cream.
   - ❏ chicken or pasta.

8. Fruits include
   - ❏ apples and cheese.
   - ❏ oranges and bananas.

9. Vegetables include
   - ❏ lettuce and tomato.
   - ❏ lemon and cucumber.

10. Meat includes
    - ❏ steak.
    - ❏ bread.

How many questions did you answer correctly? Circle your score. Then fill in your score on the Score Chart on page 91.

Number Correct	1	2	3	4	5	6	7	8	9	10
Score	10	20	30	40	50	60	70	80	90	100

Circle.

1. apple   chicken   fish

2. banana   tomato   bread

3. lettuce   cucumber   potato

4. orange   fish   cake

5. eggs   chicken   bananas

C. Practicing Vocabulary: Foods

Match.

1. cheese

2. soup

3. salad

4. pasta

5. sandwich

Complete the sentences. Use words from the box. The first one has been done for you.

apples	eggs
bananas	fish
bread	oranges
carrots	potatoes
chicken	tomatoes

1. Sandwiches have __*bread*__.

2. How much is the _____?

3. Oranges and _____ are good for you.

4. There are _____ in my salad.

5. I like _____.

6. Many people like to eat meat and _____.

7. Many people like juice from _____.

8. You can have a _____ sandwich.

9. These _____ are on sale.

10. Potatoes and _____ are vegetables.

Complete the pyramid. Write the names of some foods.

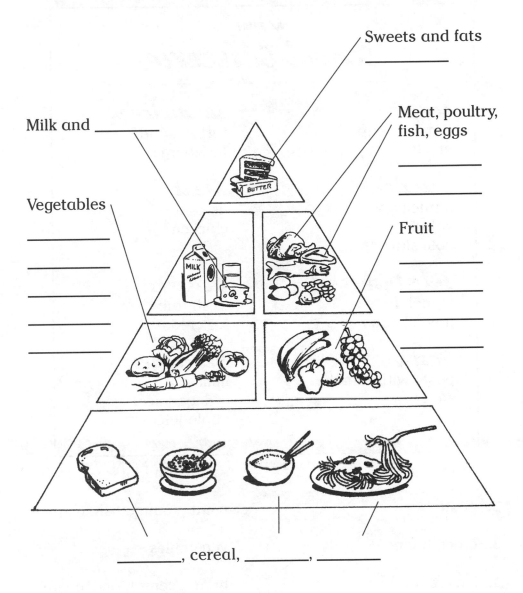

Sweets and fats
_____

Milk and _____

Meat, poultry,
fish, eggs

_____

_____

Vegetables

_____

_____

_____

Fruit

_____

_____

_____

_____

_____

_____, cereal, _____, _____

Match. The first one has been done for you.

Menu
School Cafeteria

Soup
tomato soup
chicken soup with rice

Sandwiches
turkey sandwich
hamburger

Salads
lettuce and tomato
salad
cole slaw

Meat
fish sticks
chicken

Side Dishes
French fries
green beans

Desserts
fresh fruit
ice cream

Pasta
pasta with tomato
sauce

Beverages
milk
orange juice
apple juice

---

1. orange juice   sweets and fats

2. pasta   meat, poultry, fish, eggs

3. green beans   vegetables

4. ice cream   bread, cereal, rice, pasta

5. chicken   fruit

Look at the menu on page 48. Write a meal for yourself.

_____

_____

_____

_____

TRY IT

Read the conversation.

Work with a partner. Order your meal.

WRAP-UP: WRITING AND SHARING

A. What are your favorite foods? Make a list.

_____   _____

_____   _____

_____   _____

_____   _____

Share your list with the class.

B. Interview a partner. Write your partner's favorite foods.

Partner's name: _____

_____   _____

_____   _____

C. Work with a partner. Look at your meal on page 49. Write the names of the food groups.

What food groups are in your meal? Is your meal good for you?

_____   _____

_____   _____

_____   _____

_____   _____

Let's Celebrate

We all enjoy getting together with family or friends.
What is your favorite celebration?

Your teacher will read aloud this poem about a special event.
Listen and follow along.

Celebration

by Alonzo Lopez

I shall dance tonight.
When the dusk comes crawling,
There will be dancing
       and feasting.
I shall dance with the others
     in circles,
       in leaps,
         in stomps.

Laughter and talk
     will weave into the night,
Among the fires of my people.
Games will be played
And I shall be
     a part of it.

READING INVITATIONS

Read the invitation below.

Join The Fun
Food, Art, Music, and Much More!

- Who: Students and Parents
- What: Parents' Night
- When: Thursday, May 19, 6 P.M.
- Where: Our School

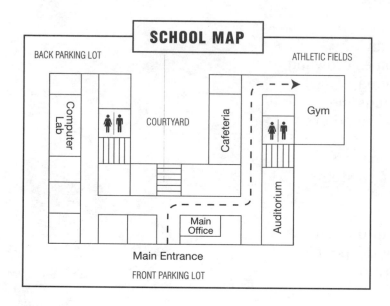

SCHOOL MAP

BACK PARKING LOT

ATHLETIC FIELDS

Computer Lab

COURTYARD

Cafeteria

Gym

Auditorium

Main Office

Main Entrance

FRONT PARKING LOT

Read the directions and study the map.

Go in through the main entrance of the school.
Walk past the main office and turn right.
Walk straight ahead to the auditorium. Turn left.
Walk past the cafeteria.
Turn right at the end of the hall.
Go into the gym.

Note:
who = people
when = time
where = place

WORDS TO LEARN

Study the words.

Direction Words

left   right   straight ahead

Action Words

turn   walk

Places

auditorium
hall
computer lab
cafeteria
apartment

entrance   office

Events

party
dinner party
Parents' Night

birthday   graduation

Months of the Year

January
February
March
April
May
June
July
August
September
October
November
December

COMPREHENSION AND VOCABULARY

A. Checking Your Understanding

Put an *x* in the box next to the correct answer. The first one has been done for you.

1. *What*, in the invitation, means
   ☒ Parents' Night.
   ❏ our school.

2. *Who*, in the invitation, means
   ❏ 6:00 P.M.
   ❏ students and parents.

3. *Where*, in the invitation, means
   ❏ students and parents.
   ❏ our school.

4. *When*, in the invitation, means
   ❏ 6:00 P.M.
   ❏ students and parents.

5. Look at the directions under the map. You go past the main office. Then you
   ❏ turn right.
   ❏ turn left.

6. You go to the auditorium. Then you
   ❏ turn right.
   ❏ turn left.

7. You walk past the cafeteria. Then you are at
   ❏ the computer lab.
   ❏ the end of the hall.

8.
   ❏ left
   ❏ right

9.
   ❏ entrance
   ❏ auditorium

10.
    ❏ birthday
    ❏ office

How many questions did you answer correctly? Circle your score. Then fill in your score on the Score Chart on page 91.

Number Correct	1	2	3	4	5	6	7	8	9	10
Score	10	20	30	40	50	60	70	80	90	100

B. Practicing Vocabulary: Question Words

Match. The first one has been done for you.

1. Who   Dinner

2. What   Friday, September 10, 7:00 P.M.

3. When   Philip's house

4. Where   Students in our English class

C. Practicing Vocabulary: Question Words

Complete the invitation. Use the words in the box.

Who   Where   When   What

_____: *Ali's friends and family*

_____: *A graduation party*

_____: *Ali's house*

_____: *Sunday, June 12, 2:00 P.M.*

Write the names of the months in order.

January					
	1	2	3	4	5
6	7	8	9	10	11	12
13	14	15	16	17	18	19

Feb_ _ _ _ _ _
						1	2
3	4	5	6	7	8	9
10	11	12	13	14	15	16

M_ _ _ _ _
						1	2
3	4	5	6	7	8	9
10	11	12	13	14	15	16

_ _ _ _ _
	1	2	3	4	5	6
7	8	9	10	11	12	13
14	15	16	17	18	19	20

M_ _
		1	2	3	4
5	6	7	8	9	10	11
12	13	14	15	16	17	18

J_ _ _
							1
2	3	4	5	6	7	8
9	10	11	12	13	14	15

_ _ _ _ _
	1	2	3	4	5	6
7	8	9	10	11	12	13

_ _ _ _ _ _
				1	2	3
4	5	6	7	8	9	10

Sept_ _ _ _ _ _
1	2	3	4	5	6	7
8	9	10	11	12	13	14

O_ _ _ _ _ _
	1	2	3	4	5
6	7	8	9	10	11	12
13	14	15	16	17	18	19
20	21	22	23	24	25	26
27	28	29	30	31

November						
					1	2
3	4	5	6	7	8	9
10	11	12	13	14	15	16
17	18	19	20	21	22	23
24	25	26	27	28	29	30

D_ _ _ _ _ _
1	2	3	4	5	6	7
8	9	10	11	12	13	14
15	16	17	18	19	20	21
22	23	24	25	26	27	28
29	30	31

Circle the months. The first one has been done for you. Write them in order on the lines below.

1. M R C (APRIL) J U

2. N O F E B R U A R Y O

3. J A N P O C J U L Y

4. M A R C H M A J U N

5. S E P O C T O B E R N O

6. D E C E M B E R A U G

7. J N A U G U S T N O V

8. S P T M A Y J A N N O

9. A P S E P T E M B E R F E

10. O C T J U N O V E M B E R

11. M A J U N E M B E R

12. J U L J A N U A R Y O C

1. _____   5. _____   9. _____

2. _____   6. _____   10. _____

3. _____   7. _____   11. _____

4. _____   8. _____   12. _____

E. Understanding Vocabulary: Directions

Read the directions. Circle *yes* or *no*. The first one has been done for you.

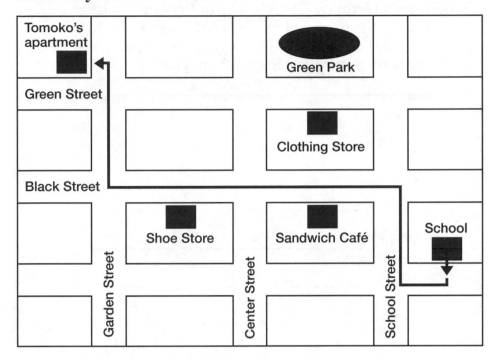

Juanita is at school.

She wants to go to Tomoko's apartment for dinner.

1. Juanita turns right at School Street.   (yes)   no

2. She turns left at Black Street.   yes   no

3. She goes straight ahead down Black Street. yes   no

4. She goes past the Sandwich Café.   yes   no

5. She turns left at Garden Street.   yes   no

6. She goes to Green Park.   yes   no

7. Tomoko's apartment is on Green Street.   yes   no

Read about Dorothy's birthday. Then complete the invitation.

It's Dorothy's birthday. There's a birthday party for her. Dorothy's friends are coming. The party is at Dorothy's apartment. Her address is 375 Spring Street, Apartment 2B. The party is on Saturday, March 12, at 5 P.M.

Who: _____

What: _____

When: _____

Where: _____

Complete the directions to Dorothy's apartment.

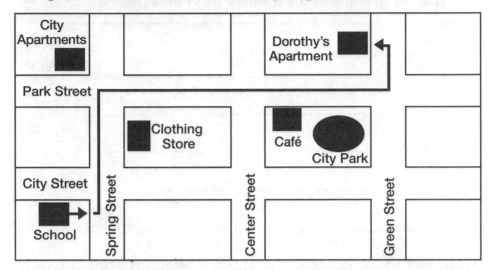

Go out through the side entrance of the school.

Turn _____ onto Spring Street.

Go past the _____.

Turn _____ on Park Street.

Walk straight _____ down Park Street.

Go past the _____.

Turn left on _____ Street.

Dorothy's apartment is on your left.

TRY IT

Work with a partner. Give directions from Dorothy's apartment to City Apartments.

WRAP-UP: WRITING AND SHARING

A. Write an invitation for a party at your house.

Who: _____

What: _____

When: _____

Where: _____

B. Share birth dates with the class. How many students were born in each month?

C. Work with a partner. Write directions from your school to a place. Draw a map.

_____

_____

_____

_____

_____

Family Fitness

What do you do to stay healthy?
Good health is important to you and your family.
Getting along with everyone is important too.

Your teacher will read aloud this poem about a family problem.
Listen and follow along.

The Quarrel
by Eleanor Farjeon

I quarreled with my brother,
I don't know what about,
One thing led to another
And somehow we fell out.
The start of it was slight,
The end of it was strong,
He said he was right,
I knew he was wrong!

We hated one another.
The afternoon turned black.
Then suddenly my brother
Thumped me on the back,
And said, "Oh, come along!
We can't go on all night—
I was in the wrong."
So he was in the right.

READING ABOUT HEALTH PROBLEMS

Read about how to treat a cold. Then read the health chart.

Phil Lopez is sick. He has a cold.
He can look in a medical book for help.
For a bad cold, he can go to the doctor's office.

Medical Book

How to treat a cold

1. Stay in bed.

2. Drink liquids.

3. Call a doctor if you feel worse.

Name _____Lopez, Phil_____

Date of Birth _____December 4, 1959_____

Reason for Visit _____Cold_____

Family History

Father: Name _____Martin_____   Age __75__

Check problems:
☒ heart problems   ❑ cancer   ❑ other

Mother: Name _____Maria_____   Age __74__

Check problems:
❑ heart problems   ❑ cancer   ❑ other

If you are married, complete this part.

Husband/Wife   Name _____Elena_____   Age __41__

Children   Name _____Mario_____   Age __17__

               Name _____Marta_____   Age __13__

               Name _____Guadalupe_____   Age __10__

WORDS TO LEARN

Study the words.

Parts of the Body

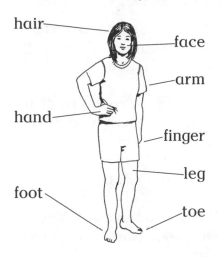

hair
face
arm
hand
finger
leg
foot
toe

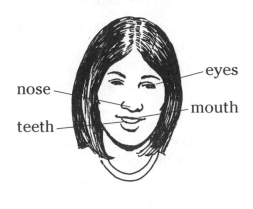

nose
eyes
mouth
teeth

Illnesses

cold

sore throat

backache

stomachache

headache

toothache

Doctors
doctor = M.D.
dentist = D.D.S.
eye doctor (optometrist) = O.D.

Other Words
medical
cancer

COMPREHENSION AND VOCABULARY

Put an *x* in the box next to the correct answer.

1. When you have a cold, it is a good idea to
   ❏ stay in bed.
   ❏ exercise.

2. When you have a cold,
   ❏ do not eat or drink.
   ❏ drink liquids.

3. Phil Lopez has a
   ❏ bad cold.
   ❏ heart problem.

4. Phil Lopez has an appointment with the
   ❏ doctor.
   ❏ dentist.

5. Phil Lopez has
   ❏ four children.
   ❏ three children.

6. Phil Lopez's father has
   ❏ a heart problem.
   ❏ cancer.

7. Phil Lopez's date of birth is
   ❏ September 5, 1959.
   ❏ December 4, 1959.

8. When you have a problem with your teeth, you go to the
   ❏ dentist.
   ❏ optometrist.

9. When you have a problem with your eyes, you go to the
   ❏ dentist.
   ❏ optometrist.

10. When you have a bad cold, you go to the
    ❏ dentist.
    ❏ doctor.

How many questions did you answer correctly? Circle your score. Then fill in your score on the Score Chart on page 91.

Number Correct	1	2	3	4	5	6	7	8	9	10
Score	10	20	30	40	50	60	70	80	90	100

Write the names of the parts of the body. Use the words in the box.

arm   face   finger   foot   hair   leg   toe   hand

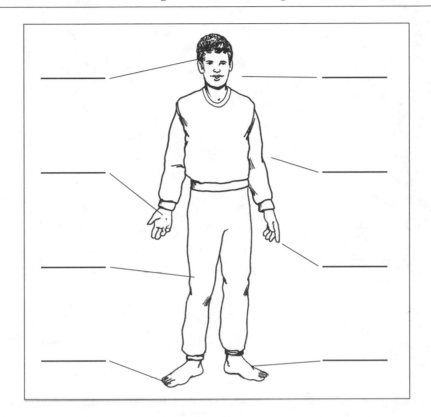

Write the names of the parts of the face. Use the words in the box.

eyes   mouth   nose   teeth

C. Practicing Vocabulary: Illnesses

Match.

1.   stomachache

2.   cold

3.   headache

4.   sore throat

5.   backache

6.    toothache

D. Practicing Vocabulary: Illnesses

Complete the sentences. Use the words in the box.

cold	headache	stomachache	toothache

1. Inez ate too much food. Now she has a _____.
2. Ricardo is sick. He has a cough and runny nose.
   He has a _____.
3. Yoko is going to the dentist.
   She has a _____.
4. I cannot think very well right now. I have a _____.

Study the Lopez family tree.

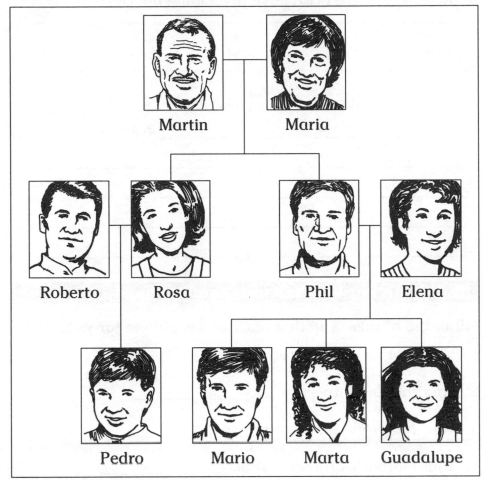

Martin   Maria

Roberto   Rosa   Phil   Elena

Pedro   Mario   Marta   Guadalupe

Note: parents = mother and father

Circle *yes* or *no*. The first one has been done for you.

1. Elena is Guadalupe's mother.   (yes)   no

2. Martin is Guadalupe's grandfather.   yes   no

3. Rosa is Guadalupe's aunt.   yes   no

4. Mario is Guadalupe's brother.   yes   no

5. Marta is Guadalupe's cousin.   yes   no

6. Phil and Elena are Guadalupe's parents.   yes   no

7. Roberto is Guadalupe's cousin.   yes   no

8. Pedro is Guadalupe's cousin.   yes   no

F. Practicing Vocabulary: Family Words

Write the family words in the correct column. Use the words in the box. The first two have been done for you.

mother	brother	son	uncle	wife
daughter	father	sister	husband	aunt

Man	Woman
father	*mother*
_____	_____
_____	_____
_____	_____

G. Practicing Vocabulary: Family Words

Fill in the blanks. The first one has been done for you.

1. Your mother's mother is your *grandmother*.

2. Your father's father is your _____.

3. Your father's sister is your _____.

4. Your mother's brother is your _____.

5. Your mother's husband is your _____.

6. Your aunt's son is your _____.

TRY IT

Work with a partner. Talk about Phil Lopez and his family. Use sentences like "Phil's father is Martin."

Read about Lin's family.

My Family

My name is Lin. I live in the United States. I am Chinese.

My father, Jialu, and my mother, Lihui, were born in China. They moved to the United States. My sister, Wei, and I were born in the United States.

My father's parents still live in China. I sometimes talk to my grandfather Yi and to my grandmother Hua. We talk on the phone.

My father has one brother, Ming. Ming lives in the United States too. Ming and his wife, Bai, have one daughter. Her name is Qian.

Complete Lin's family tree.

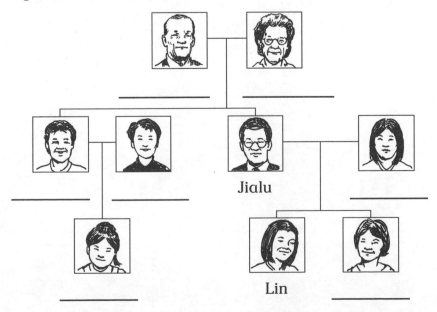

Jialu

Lin

WRAP-UP: Writing and Sharing

A. Draw your family tree or draw the family tree of some- one you know well.

Share your tree with a partner.

B. What do you do when you have a cold? What do you do when you have a headache? Tell a partner.

Checking Out the News

Newspapers contain lots of information.
They have stories about sports, concerts, other events, and the weather.
What are you interested in?

Your teacher will read aloud this poem about the newspaper.
Listen and follow along.

In the Newspaper
by G. J. Hamel

Whose team lost the game and whose team won?
Tomorrow is it going to snow?
Every day before the day's begun
I read the news I need to know
In the newspaper.

I read the headlines then the articles,
To look for things I want to do.
Concerts, circuses, or carnivals—
I find out where and when and who
In the newspaper.

Sometimes life is hard to figure out.
So if you want to find some clues,
There's a lot that you can learn about,
So many things from which to choose
In the newspaper.

READING NEWS STORIES

Read the news and weather.

Today's Weather
Sunny and hot

Temperatures:
high in the 80s

Tomorrow's Weather
Morning:
rainy and cool.
Afternoon:
cloudy and cool.
The morning will be
rainy, but the rain will
stop in the afternoon.

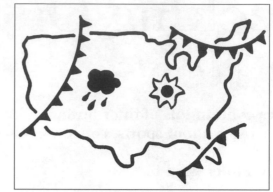

Weather for the next five days:
mostly sunny—high in the 60s.

50,000 at Concert in the Park

Yesterday evening about 50,000 people went to the free concert in the park. The large crowd of people heard music by the rock group The Brothers and Sisters. It was the largest crowd in the history of the city.

The concert began at 7 o'clock in the evening, and it ended at 9 o'clock. The group played fifteen of their songs.

The weather was good. The temperature was in the 70s. It was warm, and there was no rain.

"The music was good. I had a great time!" said Amy Childs, 18, one of the people at the concert.

"It was a great crowd," said Michael Stein of The Brothers and Sisters. "The people gave us a warm welcome."

Note: 50,000 = fifty thousand

WORDS TO LEARN

Study the words.

Weather

   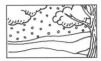

| sunny | cloudy | rainy | snowy |

Temperatures

       cold   cool   warm   hot

0°F.   30°   50° 70°   85°

Seasons

 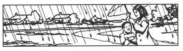

    winter   spring

    summer   fall

Time Words

yesterday	today	tomorrow
last (night)	now	next (week)
past	present	future

Actions

Present	**Past**	**Present**	**Past**
I go	I went	we go	we went
you go	you went	you go	you went
he goes	he went	they go	they went
she goes	she went		
it goes	it went		

More Clothing Words

| coat | raincoat | shorts | sunglasses | umbrella |

COMPREHENSION AND VOCABULARY

A. Checking Your Understanding

Put an *x* in the box next to the correct answer.

Look at the newspaper articles on page 72.

1. What is the weather like today?
   - ❏ sunny and hot
   - ❏ sunny and cold

2. What will the weather be like tomorrow?
   - ❏ rainy
   - ❏ mostly sunny

3. Where was the concert?
   - ❏ at 7 o'clock
   - ❏ at the park

4. When was the concert?
   - ❏ at 7 o'clock
   - ❏ the afternoon

5. What was the weather like at the concert?
   - ❏ rainy
   - ❏ warm

6. The number of people at the concert was about
   - ❏ 5,000
   - ❏ 50,000

7. Who played at the concert?
   - ❏ a rock group
   - ❏ the crowd

8.
   - ❏ sunny
   - ❏ cloudy

9. past
   - ❏ yesterday
   - ❏ today

10. future
   - ❏ yesterday
   - ❏ tomorrow

How many questions did you answer correctly? Circle your score. Then fill in your score on the Score Chart on page 91.

Number Correct	1	2	3	4	5	6	7	8	9	10
Score	10	20	30	40	50	60	70	80	90	100

Circle. The first one has been done for you.

1.

(sunny)   cloudy   (summer)

2.

sunny   winter   snowy

3.

fall   windy   cool

4.
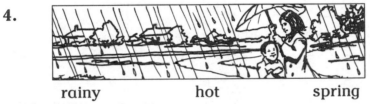

rainy   hot   spring

C. Practicing Vocabulary: Weather Words

Write about the weather for the seasons. Use the pictures above for help. The first one has been done for you.

1. In summer, it is __*hot*__ and __*sunny*__ .

2. In winter, it is _____ and _____ .

3. In fall, it is _____ and _____ .

4. In spring, it is _____ and _____ .

D. Practicing Vocabulary: Clothing

Match.

1. umbrella

2. raincoat

3. coat

4. sunglasses

5. shorts

E. Practicing Vocabulary: Clothing and Weather

Complete the sentences. Use the pictures. The first one has been done for you.

1.

    When it is _snowy_, you can wear a _coat_.

2.

    When it is _____, take an _____.

3.

    When I go to the _____, I take _____ to wear.

4.

    When it is _____, many people wear _____.

5.

    When it is _____, wear a _____ to stay warm.

6.

    When it is _____, I often wear a _____.

Circle. The first one has been done for you.

1. today   past   (present)   future

2. next week   past   present   future

3. last night   past   present   future

4. last Tuesday   past   present   future

5. next Tuesday   past   present   future

Circle.

1. There was a concert last night.   past   present   future

2. It will rain tomorrow.   past   present   future

3. It is raining now.   past   present   future

4. Next week there will be a soccer game.   past   present   future

5. Yesterday it was hot.   past   present   future

6. Today it is cool.   past   present   future

G. Read and Write

Look at the weather map.

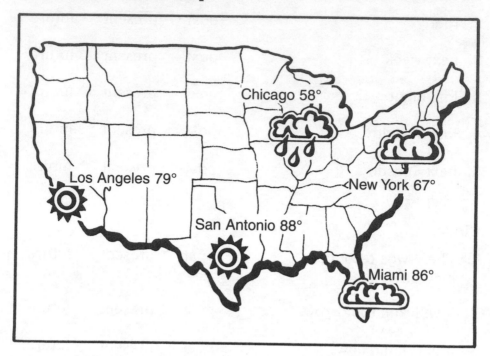

Complete the sentences. The first one has been done for you.

1. In Los Angeles, the weather is _sunny_ and _warm_.

2. In Chicago, the weather is _____ and _____.

3. In New York, it is _____ and _____.

4. In Miami, it is _____ and _____.

5. In San Antonio, it is _____ and _____.

TRY IT

Work with a partner. Use the map. Tell about the weather in the cities.

Read the news story.

U.S. Will Play Brazil in City Stadium

A Large Crowd Will Fill City Stadium

Next week two famous soccer teams will come to our city. The national team of the United States will play the national team of Brazil.

City Stadium

Many soccer fans will come to our city for the game. More than 40,000 people will be in City Stadium. It will be the largest crowd in the history of the stadium.

U.S. Team, Brazil Team

The game is next Sunday at 4:00 in the afternoon. You can buy tickets for the game at City Stadium. The cost is $30.00 for one ticket. There are about 5,000 tickets left.

Write the answer to each question. Use the information in the news story. the first one has been done for you.

1. What will happen?   *A soccer game*
   _____

2. Who will play?   _____

3. Who will come?   _____

4. When will the game be?   _____

5. Where will the game be?   _____

6. How much money does a ticket cost?   _____

WRAP-UP: WRITING AND SHARING

A. Answer the questions.

1. Work with a partner. What is the weather like today?

_____

_____

2. Work with a partner. What was the weather like yesterday?

_____

_____

3. Get a newspaper from your city. Work with a partner. What will the weather be like tomorrow?

_____

_____

B. Answer and share.

1. What is the weather like in your country of origin?

_____

_____

2. Share with the class.

Television Rules!

What are your favorite TV shows?
Do you watch game shows, soap operas, or mysteries?
You can find them all in the TV listings.

Your teacher will read aloud this poem about watching TV.
Listen and follow along.

Talking Television
by Ken Fontenot

Mom tells me that to her the TV
looks like a sunny window.

Dad watches mostly sports and news.
Sometimes I see him fall asleep
in his easy chair, the TV on. I like
to think he's dreaming he's a football star.

As for me, I want to be a fast-talking host
and listen to my guests surprise us all.

READING TV LISTINGS

TV Listings.

Read to see what will be on TV.

Channel 2	**Channel 3**
6:00 P.M.	
News	Cooking Show
Channel 2 News at 6:00 P.M. Hear all the news from the city and from around the world.	***Mario's Kitchen*** How to make vegetable soup. Mario gives his family's recipe for vegetable soup. 
7:00 P.M.	
Talk Show	Soap Opera
The Barbara Lane Show The rock group The Brothers and Sisters are guests. They will talk about their new songs. The host is Barbara Lane. 	***Life in the City*** Three young women—Linda, Sue, and Tina—share an apartment. They also share problems with money and boyfriends. Today Linda introduces her new boyfriend. What's the problem? He was Tina's boyfriend last year.
8:00 P.M.	
Comedy	Drama
Phil's Problems People remembered Phil's birthday, but everybody gave him the same present. he now has 10 copies of the same CD. What will he do? You will laugh.	***Dinosaurs!*** People go back to the time of the dinosaurs. 
9:00 P.M.	
Music Videos	Sports
The Newest Songs All the newest songs are here from your favorite music groups.	***Basketball Game*** The Chicago Bulls play the San Antonio Spurs.

WORDS TO LEARN

Study the words.

Kinds of TV Programs

news
comedy
drama
soap opera
commercial

Other TV Words

channel
TV program
TV show
watch TV

Time Words

before
after

9:00 A.M. ◄——— (10:00 A.M.) ———► 11:00 A.M.

before 10:00 A.M.   after 10:00 A.M.

Other Words

boyfriend
girlfriend

Note:
cook   = make food
recipe = directions for making food
host   = person who gives an invitation

CD

COMPREHENSION AND VOCABULARY

A. Checking Your Understanding

Put an *x* in the box next to the correct answer.

1. What time is the news on TV?
   - ❏ 6:00 P.M.
   - ❏ 9:00 P.M.

2. What channel is the news on?
   - ❏ Channel 2
   - ❏ Channel 3

3. What program is on at 8:00 P.M.?
   - ❏ Phil's Problems
   - ❏ Music Videos

4. What program is a soap opera?
   - ❏ Life in the City
   - ❏ Dinosaurs!

5. The drama at 8:00 P.M. is about
   - ❏ CDs.
   - ❏ dinosaurs.

6. The sports program at 9:00 P.M. is a
   - ❏ basketball game.
   - ❏ soccer game.

7. *Phil's Problems* is a
   - ❏ comedy.
   - ❏ drama.

8. The women in *Life in the City* have problems with
   - ❏ school.
   - ❏ boyfriends.

9. 7:00 P.M. comes _____ 8:00 P.M.
   - ❏ before
   - ❏ after

10. 2:00 P.M. comes _____ 1:00 P.M.
    - ❏ before
    - ❏ after

How many questions did you answer correctly? Circle your score. Then fill in your score on the Score Chart on page 91.

Number Correct	1	2	3	4	5	6	7	8	9	10
Score	10	20	30	40	50	60	70	80	90	100

Read the TV listings below.

Channel 4	Channel 5
4:00 P.M.	
Soap Opera ***Boyfriends and Girlfriends***	News
5:00 P.M.	
News	Comedy ***Maria's World***
6:00 P.M.	
Cooking Show How to make tomato sauce for pasta.	Soccer Game The United States plays Canada.
7:00 P.M.	
Movie/Drama ***A Doctor's Life***	Soccer Game—continued

Complete the sentences with *before* or *after*. The first one has been done for you.

1. On Channel 4, there is a cooking show ___*after*___ the news.

2. On Channel 5, there is a comedy show _____ the news.

3. On Channel 4, there is a soap opera _____ the news.

4. On Channel 5, there is a soccer game _____ the comedy.

5. On Channel 4, there is a drama _____ the cooking show.

TRY IT

Work with a partner. Look at the TV listings in the newspaper. Tell about the programs.

Read the TV listings below.

| Channel 6 | Channel 7 |

6:00 P.M.

News

The Day in the News
Richard Jones gives you the
news of the world and of the
city.

Soap Opera

Joy and Sadness
The members of a family
try to reach their goals.
Their lives are difficult, but
they are brave people.

7:00 P.M.

Comedy

Life in the Family
The parents and children
change places for a day.
The children go to work.
Who has the most
problems?

Drama

Into the Future
A woman goes on a visit to
the future.

8:00 P.M.

Cooking Show

Adriana at Home
Adriana makes bread.

Movie Talk Show

Flora and Fred at the Movies
Flora and Fred talk about all
the new movies.

9:00 P.M.

Drama

In Love
A young man in his 20s falls
in love with a woman in her
40s. What will happen?

Sports

World Soccer
The United States plays
Brazil.

Read the conversation.

> I watch TV most weeknights. I like dramas and soap operas. I don't like sports, and I don't like programs in which people sit and talk.

> I watch TV about one night a week. I like to watch the news. I really like comedies, but I like sports the best.

Answer the questions.

What programs on page 86 will Alejandra watch?

_____

_____

_____

What programs will Deshon watch?

_____

_____

_____

D. What programs do you want to watch?

Write the names of the TV programs you want to watch.

_____

_____

_____

TRY IT

Work with a partner. Tell about the kinds of TV shows you like.

Read the story below.

Soap Operas

Many people like to watch soap operas on TV. Soap operas tell stories about families. They tell stories about people's personal lives. Usually the people in soap operas have problems.

Here is one story from a soap opera.

Javier is in his junior year of high school. He has two sisters, Nicolasa and Maura. Several months ago, an exchange student came to live with his family. Her name is Elena. She is from El Salvador.

Elena and Nicolasa are both seniors in high school. They are planning to attend the prom. No boy asked Elena to go to the prom. Nicolasa asked Javier to take Elena to the prom. Javier said yes. Elena is very excited. She and Nicolasa are looking for prom dresses.

Javier likes a girl at school named Rosita. Rosita is a senior. Javier and Rosita sometimes talk during lunch. Javier thinks that Rosita likes him, but he is not sure. One day Rosita sees Javier in the hallway. She asks him if he will go to the prom with her. Javier says yes. He is very happy.

E. Read and Write

Javier is not happy when he gets home. He had forgotten what he told Nicolasa. He is supposed to go to the prom with Elena. He remembers now. Javier goes to ask his father for advice. Javier's father is not happy. He tells his son to do what is right.

Javier really wants to go to the prom with Rosita. Javier knows that he should go with Elena. He does not want his father and sister to be angry. He does not want Elena to be sad. He does not want Rosita to be sad.

What will Javier do?

Watch the soap opera *Joy and Sadness* to find out.

Circle *yes* or *no*. The first one has been done for you.

1. Javier has two sisters.   (yes)   no

2. Elena is from Cuba.   yes   no

3. Javier is a senior in high school   yes   no

4. Elena wants to go to the prom.   yes   no

5. Rosita is Javier's sister.   yes   no

WRAP-UP: WRITING AND SHARING

A. What are your favorite kinds of TV programs? Make a list.

_____

_____

_____

Share your list with a partner.

B. What kinds of TV programs do you watch? Write the kinds for each day for the next week.

Sunday	Monday	Tuesday	Wednesday	Thursday	Friday	Saturday

Share your list with the class. Which kinds of programs do most students like? Write them below.

_____

_____

_____

SCORE CHART

This is the Score Chart for Comprehension and Vocabulary. Shade in your score for each unit. For example, if your score was 80 for **Letters and Numbers,** look at the bottom of the chart for **Letters and Numbers.** Shade in the bar up to the 80 mark. By looking at this chart, you can see how well you did on each unit.

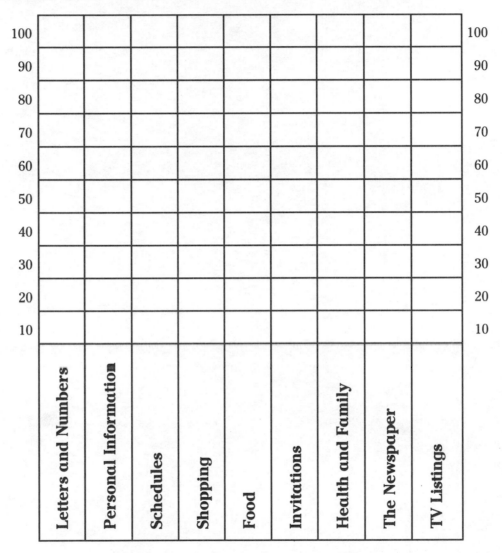